Spotted Owl

Bird of the Ancient Forest

Here's a list of other nonfiction
Redfeather Books from Henry Holt

Alligators: A Success Story
by Patricia Lauber

Earthworms: Underground Farmers
by Patricia Lauber

*Exploring an Ocean Tide Pool
by Jeanne Bendick

Frozen Man
by David Getz

*Great Whales: The Gentle Giants
by Patricia Lauber

Salmon Story
by Brenda Z. Guiberson

*Snakes: Their Place in the Sun
by Robert M. McClung

*Available in paperback

SPOTTED OWL

Bird of the Ancient Forest

BRENDA Z. GUIBERSON

With illustrations by the author

A Redfeather Book

HENRY HOLT AND COMPANY • NEW YORK

The author wishes to thank Joe Buchanan
and Malcolm North for their insight,
information, and review of the
working manuscript for this book.

Henry Holt and Company, Inc.
Publishers since 1866
115 West 18th Street
New York, New York 10011

Henry Holt is a registered
trademark of Henry Holt and Company, Inc.

Library of Congress Cataloging-in-Publication Data
Guiberson, Brenda Z.
Spotted owl, bird of the ancient forest / Brenda Z. Guiberson;
with illustrations by the author.
p.   cm.—(A Redfeather book)
1. Spotted owl—Northwest, Pacific—Juvenile literature.
2. Forest ecology—Northwest, Pacific—Juvenile literature.
3. Old-growth forests—Northwest, Pacific—Juvenile literature.
4. Lumber trade—Environmental aspects—Northwest, Pacific—Juvenile
literature. [1. Spotted owl.   2. Owls.   3. Old-growth forests.
4. Lumber and lumbering.   5. Forest ecology.   6. Ecology.]
I. Title.   II. Series: Redfeather books.
QL696.S83G84   1994   94-13888

ISBN 0-8050-3171-5
First Edition—1994
Printed in the United States of America
on acid-free paper.∞

1   3   5   7   9   10   8   6   4   2

To that community of friends,
linked together and developing
for so many years:
Nadine Boettcher, Laurie Dunn,
Bonnie Halbert, Judy Hall,
Debbie Kari, Mary Peters,
Sharon Prueitt, Jean Rempel,
Sandy Sanders, Lolly Smith.

Contents

SPOTTED OWL

Bird of the Ancient Forest

1

❧

Who's
in the Forest?

The spotted owl is a rare bird that spends quiet days asleep in some of the biggest trees in the Pacific Northwest. At times this bird is curious and talkative; it can hoot at other owls in at least thirteen different ways. The spotted owl likes to eat flying squirrels in the middle of the night and has special eyes and ears to find food in the dark. Its spotted brown feathers hide it so well in the forest that for a long time no one really seemed to know it was there.

But now this bird has been discovered and has become famous to loggers, environmentalists, foresters, and politicians. The bird has shown up on bumper stickers and magazine covers and in unkind recipes for owl stew. Its living habits have even been explained to the president of the United States. Some people think this owl can save the last of the old forests of the Pacific Northwest. Others think this same bird is taking money and jobs from their families and communities.

Meanwhile the spotted owl lives quietly in the shelter of the oldest forests in Washington, Oregon, and northern California, trying to survive. Every year there are fewer and fewer spotted owls, because it is getting very difficult for this bird to find a good place to live.

What kind of place does the spotted owl need? To find out, let's take a good look at an owl in the forest.

The spotted owl is a bird that does not like to get wet. Its feathers are not waterproof, and it can get dangerously cold when soaked. So when a rain cloud blows in off the Pacific Ocean and storms over the forest, the spotted owl flies into a hole in a Douglas-fir tree. The tree is an ancient one, growing for over eight hundred years, and full of woodpecker holes and rotten places. It is just what the owl needs, because spotted owls do not make their own nests. And this old tree is important to other plants and animals in the forest too.

Just above the owl, a bat sleeps in a deep crevice of a broken limb. Ants and bright green beetles find homes under the rough bark. A chipmunk with a mouthful of mushroom scurries up the trunk to a dry spot under a huge mossy branch. A mouselike animal called a vole nibbles on the soft center of a fir needle. Higher still, a female owl and a baby owlet sit quietly in a deep hole made when the top of the tree broke off in a storm.

Amazingly, there are over sixty million needles on this great tree. The rain slows down as it drips from them in its fall through the forest. Some of the water never reaches the ground, as it soaks into all the thick clumps of moss, lichen, and mistletoe on the tree.

Some rain drizzles through hemlock and cedar trees growing in the shade of the Douglas fir. As the storm builds up force over the ocean, all these trees inside the forest slow the wind and the pelting rain. A deer from a nearby meadow runs deep into the forest to find shelter from the storm.

The rain drips onto the snags, the standing dead trees full of more rotten places and woodpecker holes. Then it falls onto a Pacific yew, a slow-growing tree with bright red bark, and plops onto some vine maples, sword ferns, and berry bushes. Finally the rain soaks into the crumbling wood of fallen logs on the ground. As the rain sifts through all the plant layers of the forest, it comes out clean and clear and trickles into the nearby stream, flowing over the salmon and salamanders, frogs and insects that live in the water. This soaking and filtering of the water is important to every creature that depends on clean fresh water to live in or to drink.

Hoo . . . hoo-hoo . . . hoooo. When the rain stops, another spotted owl flies into this part of the forest and hoots. He is a young owl, looking for a place to live. The adult owl in the fir tree answers and flies out to see who has come into his territory. When the younger owl hears the call, he knows that this area of the forest is already taken and flaps off through the trees.

As the sun sets, an elk steps from the shelter of a great cedar and breaks off a young tree sapling to eat. A yellow banana slug leaves a trail of mucus as it makes a slow trip across a wet log.

When it gets dark, the male spotted owl swoops sixty feet down to a low branch on the Pacific yew tree. Here the owl prepares to sit and wait, sit and wait, until an animal comes by that it would like for dinner.

As the owl perches, great numbers of bats flap out of their hiding places behind the thick bark of old trees. They fly over the stream with mouths open, skimming the clear water for a drink. Then they eat mosquitoes and moths and fly off to roost in the forest. As they leave, a flying squirrel leaps from a cedar tree and glides silently on its extra flaps of skin to the forest floor.

The owl still waits patiently on the branch of the yew. He twists his head in a circle when he hears a familiar rustling near the fallen log below. He often hunts in places like this because the log is a dead piece of wood that is full of life. It has been on the ground for centuries and is over two hundred feet long. A salamander lives in a hollow in the soft, damp wood, and not far away is a nest for voles. Spiders, ants, and termites crawl through its tiny cavities, and earthworms work below the log to turn its rotting wood into new, rich soil. Fungi and bacteria fill the holes, and mushrooms grow everywhere.

The top of this log has become a nursery for new trees and other plants to grow. There is such a thick mass of needles and moss on the floor that the trees of the forest find it easier to sprout here. Hemlock and spruce trees are growing up on this "nurse log." As the log slowly rots away, their tree roots will grow around it to reach into the ground.

The owl continues to watch quietly. He can hear very well and knows that the rustling sound near the log comes from a flying squirrel digging into the earth because she smells something to eat. She is digging up a truffle, the fruit of a fungus that grows around the roots of the great trees. The trees need the fungus because it brings nutrients to their roots to help them grow. The animals that eat truffles spread the fungus in their droppings to other trees all over the forest.

The flying squirrel finds her dinner and quickly takes

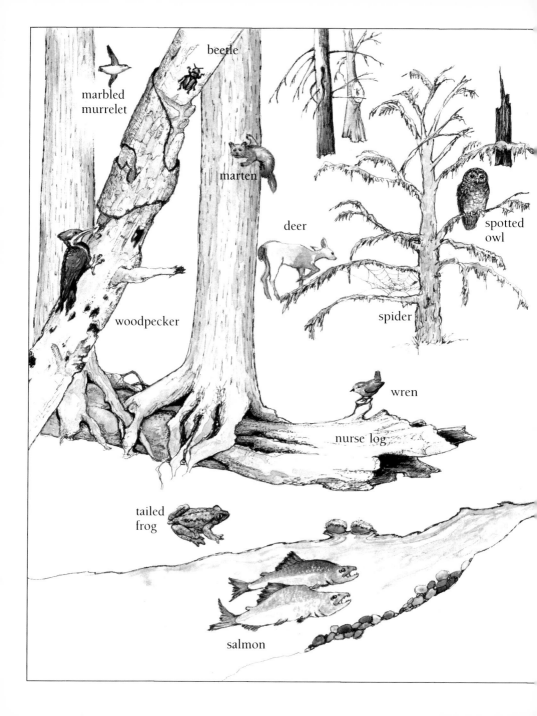

Some Plants and Animals
in an Old-Growth Forest

a few small bites. It is at this moment that the spotted owl lifts off from the nearby branch. He flies so quietly that the squirrel does not hear him come. In a flash, the owl picks up the animal with his talons and flies off to share the meal with his mate and owlet in the nest.

Not far away, a chunky little bird with short wings flaps her way through the forest. She is not a good flier because she is a seabird who is much better at floating on water and then plunging under the surface to catch fish. But this marbled murrelet was born in the ancient forest and comes back here to find a nest. She looks for a soft, thick spot where moss and lichen have been growing together for hundreds of years. This is the only type of nest that she knows, and she has flown over forty miles from the ocean to find it on an ancient tree.

This is the world that the spotted owl knows so well. It is a community of life called an old-growth forest, one that can take two hundred years to begin to develop. It contains animals that depend on trees and trees that depend on animals. It is so complex that we are just beginning to understand it when it is almost gone.

There used to be fifteen million acres of these old-growth forests where the spotted owl could live. Now ninety percent of them are gone. What happened to them? It seems that trees have been disappearing ever since people first came into the forest.

Young spotted owls resting on a tree branch near Cabin Creek, Washington. *Copyright Tracy L. Fleming.*

2

Timberrr!

The first people to come into the old-growth forests of the Pacific Northwest were the Indians. They figured out what to use for food and shelter and then left the rest of the forest alone to grow as it had been doing for thousands of years. Occasionally they burned the underbrush to allow plenty of room for berry bushes to grow, and once in a while these fires got out of control.

But mostly the Indians lived quietly and did little to disturb the spotted owl and other wildlife. They collected forest plants to eat and to use for medicine. They caught salmon in the streams. They also found good uses for the different kinds of trees, using the biggest to carve huge totem poles and great canoes that could hold sixty people.

They used the snappy wood of the Pacific yew to make bows and harpoons. Cedar was bent into boxes or split into straight pieces to make the great longhouses where they lived. They wove cedar bark into rain capes or shredded it to use as towels, torches, or kindling.

The next people to come into the forest were the settlers. They passed through many other forests in this country before getting to the Pacific Northwest. As they traveled they cut down trees and made them into ships, railroads, forts, cities, bridges, buckets, and even false teeth. As the settlers moved west, ancient forest disappeared in several parts of the country.

But nobody ever thought that this huge country would run out of trees. When the settlers finally arrived in the Pacific Northwest, they were sure of it. Here they walked into forests bigger and thicker than anything seen before.

They were not happy to see all these huge trees. They described them as "monsters," "thick as hair on the back of a dog." The forests seemed "full of wild beasts," "timber, timber, 'til you can't sleep." They thought of the trees as "weeds," worthless and in the way. They never considered the spotted owl and the other creatures that lived there. They just wanted to remove the trees so they could plant crops and build cities.

The loggers were the next people who came into the forest. They walked in with razor-sharp axes, but it still took two men several days to cut down some of these huge trees. It was dangerous work.

Early twentieth-century loggers join hands to show the size of an old-growth tree trunk, forming a chain around its base. *University of Washington Library, no. 2369.*

Tall tales were told across the country about how strong, daring, and creative loggers had to be. Paul Bunyan, the biggest and most powerful logging character of all, became a folk hero. People said that when he was only three weeks old, he did enough rolling around in his sleep to knock down four square miles of timber. Later, when he dragged a logging tool across the country, he made a little scratch that became the Grand Canyon. Things happened in big ways for Paul Bunyan.

In real life, many men died when trees fell in unexpected

places or exploded as they hit the ground. Old hollow trees were especially risky because a hinge of wood could not be left in the final cut to control the fall. Occasionally a hibernating bear with a cub or two might be found in the middle, and then everybody would leave the area in a hurry.

The loggers who cut fallen logs into smaller pieces could be crushed if the wood shifted. Others died trying to break up logs floating to sawmills that jammed up in the rivers. Some accidents happened in the mills when saw blades broke and sprang back against the workers. The average survival in this business before injury or death was only seven years.

After the trees came down, nobody wanted to take out the huge stumps left in the ground. Portland, Oregon, which in its early days was nicknamed "Stump Town," allowed people to pay off their taxes by removing stumps. Prisoners were often given a sentence that included stump removal.

As more people came west, a few of them began to realize that these logs might be worth something after all. They could see that gold miners in California and shipbuilders on the coast needed wood. When the city of San Francisco burned down in 1906, they could imagine the enormous number of logs needed to rebuild. The newest people in the woods were businessmen. They realized

A logger poses within the cut of an old-growth tree trunk, circa 1910. *University of Washington Library, no. 15170.*

that if they could get the logs out of the mountains and down to the builders, they would make a lot of money.

So the huge pines, firs, hemlocks, and cedars were no longer considered weeds. But they were not considered as a home for the spotted owl, either. These big trees were a resource waiting to be cut and sold. The thin, low-growing plants of the forest were now seen as useless and in the way. Pacific yews, alders, snowbrush, and huckle-berries became the weeds. They were pushed over, pulled out, and burned in huge slash fires.

The government made it easy for people in the timber business. Officials sold off some land as cheaply as ten or twelve cents an acre. The government also gave millions of acres to the railroads, to encourage them to build a line all across the country. When the railroads were completed, every tree close to the train tracks was cut down and hauled off on flatcars. Many old trees in the world of the spotted owl simply disappeared.

Fortunately for the spotted owl, there were other people in the forest. Hikers, hunters, tourists, and photographers were also there. They were concerned about the huge loss of trees and places where wildlife could live. Even back a hundred years ago, a timber battle was being fought be-tween the people who thought the trees should be cut and those who thought they shouldn't. One president would put millions of acres into reserves to save the trees. An-

Effects of
Heavy Logging

WIND

Young spotted owls looking for their own territory may not be able to reach this distant fragment of forest.

This island of trees may not be large enough to support a family of spotted owls.

The clear-cut area has little food or hiding places for many small animals.

In bad weather, deer and elk crowd into the remaining forest for shelter. Large numbers may damage the forest if they overeat the shrubs and tree bark.

Flying squirrels and voles will not come out into this open area to spread the fungi needed for new trees to grow.

Trees at the edge are warmer, drier, and more likely to topple over in the wind.

Old-growth climate occurs only in the center of the forest.

other president might take some of them back out for logging. But in spite of the battle, national parks and wilderness areas were gradually created as public land where people could go to enjoy the beauty of these great forests and where the spotted owl could still find a nesting place in an ancient tree.

After World War II, the country was doing so much rebuilding and growing that more wood than ever was needed. Private timber companies had already used up most of their own wood, so they began to make deals with the U.S. Forest Service to use the trees on public land. At that time foresters did not know much about old-growth forests. Some described them as "biological deserts," with all that dead wood just rotting away. Their job was to identify the acres to be cut and then build roads into the area. Now it was the dead and rotting trees that were the weeds. The loggers cut down the best wood and burned the rest. This was called clear-cut logging and was very hard on the spotted owl. Each time it was done, huge areas of trees, nests, truffles, and flying squirrels were all lost. Some of the areas were replanted with millions of new seedlings, all the same kind of trees. Unfortunately, these tree farms were not a place where the spotted owl could live either.

Old-growth logging was big business, and logging jobs were not hard to find. In many small communities, almost everyone in town had some connection to the timber business. In the state of Washington, even schools received money from the sale of timber.

But as the old-growth forests got smaller, the timber battle grew bigger. The forests were being cut at a rate much faster than trees could grow back. The Forest Service had eight times as many roads to maintain as the entire interstate highway system. The logged areas and these dirt roads were dumping tons of silt into streams in the mountains. Salmon could hardly survive in these muddy waters. Fishermen had less fish to catch and were losing jobs. They stepped into the timber battle, demanding that trees be left around the streams for the fish. But others saw no good reason to stop. Families needed jobs and people wanted lumber, paper, and plywood, didn't they?

During the 1980s, so much old-growth forest was cut that only small patches remained. Some of the patches were so far from others that they became like islands, not connected to other forests. This made it very difficult for spotted owls to travel from one fragment of forest to the next. Some of the patches were too small for the owls to find enough food to raise a family.

Meanwhile businesspeople were trying to become more efficient. They bought new machines that could snip trees at the tree farms in thirty seconds flat and then built computerized sawmills to handle the wood. Thousands

This large clear-cut shows the long edge of a remaining old-growth forest. *Copyright Michael Ichisaka.*

of timber jobs were lost as a result of these changes.

In the 1980s, the largest lumber and plywood companies reduced the number of farms they had in the Northwest and doubled what they grew in the South because there were fewer problems and trees grow fast in the heat. Thousands of additional jobs were lost by this change in the industry.

Businesspeople also discovered they could get more money for their logs by shipping them to countries in Asia that didn't have any of their own. One quarter of the logs left in ships without ever passing through the sawmills. This added up to many more lost jobs, and emotions were building to an intense level. The loggers were desperate for more logs and more jobs. The environmentalists were desperate to save the last of the old-growth forests so the spotted owl and other wildlife would have a place to live.

Meanwhile there were some new people out in the forest. This time scientists were taking a serious, microscopic look at all the forests—young, old, wet, and dry. They tried hard to understand how much wood could be cut and how much should be left for the owl. What were the weeds and what was valuable? They came up with some surprising answers.

3

❧

Old Forest, New Forest— Is There a Difference?

In 1968, a student scientist in an old-growth forest heard the hooting of an owl. He liked owls, knew a lot about them, and decided to hoot back in the same way.

Much to his surprise, the owl flew through the forest, landed nearby, and stared at him with huge, circular eyes. This was very unusual. Most of the time if a person makes a noise, every animal in the area disappears.

This time, though, a small owl with spotted brown feathers made a long, leisurely visit. It was a very rare bird, one that few had seen and no one knew anything about. And amazingly, he seemed more curious than afraid. The student began to study and write about the spotted owl, and soon everyone who wanted to know more about life in the forests heard about this bird that was willing to be seen.

Beginning in the 1970s, scientists from many different fields decided to take an expert look at the forests. Some counted salmon; others looked for fungi or insects. A few with rock-climbing equipment climbed high into the treetops for the very first time. They measured wind and rain and made detailed maps of everything growing on the trees. Some looked at slugs, bats, voles, salamanders, the marbled murrelet, and many other rare and unusual creatures.

But the creature that got studied the most was the northern spotted owl. Many scientists went into the woods to call this friendly bird. Eventually they got answers from over two thousand pairs of owls. Because these owls often come back to the same nest year after year, the scientists got to know some of them very well. One owl likes to watch from a low branch but refuses to answer. Another has a distinctly low, gruff voice and his own way of hooting, unlike any of the thirteen hoots used by other spotted owls.

Scientists continue this work, calling owls in the middle of the night when the birds are out hunting. They walk through the forest, *hoo . . . hooot*ing until they finally get an answer. If they want to find the nest or count babies, they come back in the daylight and call again. This time

A biologist prepares to band a spotted owl in Oregon. *Copyright Michael Ichisaka.*

they bring a live mouse, call, and step back. In a few moments, the owl swoops down for a meal. If the owl has a mate and a baby or two, it will fly off and take this mouse to the nest. This is why the scientists come back in the daylight, because now they must run through the forest, following the bird to its nest. By doing this, they learn where the owls live and if they are able to raise a family.

The spotted owl has been very cooperative. Not only does it answer calls and point the way to its nest, but the bird also reveals what it had for supper. Owls eat their food whole, and the parts that they can't digest, like fur and bones, get spit out in the form of pellets. Scientists collect pellets from around the nest, pull them apart, and figure out what the owl has been eating.

The owl spits up food it cannot digest as a tightly packed ball called a pellet. When the pellet is pulled apart, fur, bones, and insect parts can be seen.

The scientists have also attached radio transmitters to some of the owls. By listening for the sounds coming from the transmitters, they can learn how far the owl goes in the forest. They discovered that the spotted owl is very rare, and lives mostly in old-growth forests and almost nowhere else. This was very important because all the people who wanted to stop the logging of old forests now knew about a creature that depended on these ancient trees. If the old forests disappeared, the spotted owl would most likely become extinct. It took a long time, but finally, in 1990, the spotted owl was listed as a threatened species. The places where this bird lives were now protected by law.

Now the question became, How much area does the spotted owl need to survive? From the radio tracking, the scientists learned that owls in different forests use between a thousand and up to many thousands of acres of forest to hunt. Owls that eat mostly flying squirrels, which are small, need much more space than owls that eat mostly wood rats, which are four times bigger.

Because of the law, many acres of old-growth trees around owl nests became off-limits to logging. Nobody in the timber industry wanted this to happen. They had already lost too many jobs through other changes, and now the last of the big, valuable trees could not be cut. They wanted to know why the owl couldn't just move over to one of the tree farms or even to the zoo.

In an old-growth forest, light briefly illuminates an area of dead trees and rotting plants. *Copyright Malcolm North.*

Nobody could agree on how many acres to save for the owl, and sometimes none were being saved at all. Finally a judge ruled that there would be no more logging until a plan could be found that would protect the spotted owl as required by law.

During all of this, some scientists were still in the forest, working on special reports that would be used to help make this plan. The first thing they had to do was to carefully define an old-growth forest. For a while not everybody was talking about the same thing.

The scientists described old growth as a messy forest. It has more than one kind of tree, some small, some big, some old, and others just beginning to grow. Some of the trees are very large—or over two hundred years old. Because the trees are different ages, the forest is uneven, with high, low, and broken branches. And finally, there are plenty of snags (standing dead trees) and fallen logs on the ground.

All of this is very important to the spotted owl. An old-growth forest includes ancient trees for its nest and places where the flying squirrel can live and find truffles to eat. It also has plenty of open spaces around fallen trees where the owl can fly and low branches where it can hunt. The owl also moves between high and low branches as a way to warm up or cool off.

Once the scientists determined exactly what old growth

was, they also knew what it wasn't. They discovered that there are connections between plants and animals in an old forest that don't really develop until the trees are about two hundred years old. They found many plants and animals in addition to the spotted owl that depend on these connections for all or part of their lives. What is it about an old forest that makes it so different from a young one?

Every so often, a big disaster occurs in a forest that kills some or all of the trees. It might be caused by a fire, wind, a volcano, disease, or maybe too many insects. Because these disasters happen all the time, there are forests of different types and ages all over the landscape.

After a natural disaster, a forest will grow back. Fortunately for the spotted owl, often not all the trees are lost. For instance, lightning might kill a tall tree and start a "cool fire"—a fire that burns through the small plants on the ground. But the ancient trees are protected by bark that is twelve or even fifteen inches thick. Some of the old trees will survive to reseed the forest. The owl and others will still have big trees available for nests, food, and perching, and the trees will still have the small animals to spread the fungi that help new trees to grow.

Sometimes a forest will go through a bigger change. The most drastic thing that can happen is clear-cut logging, where every single tree is cut down, with the valuable ones taken to a sawmill and the others burned. In clear-

A hiker walks by tree trunks still charred from a forest fire seven years earlier. *Copyright Ted Thomas.*

cut logging, the animals lose everything.

The law now requires replanting of clear-cut areas. Each year billions of tree seedlings are put into the ground to grow as a tree farm. One farm might be planted with Douglas fir, a valuable wood for building. Another farm might be planted with cottonwood or poplar to make into pulp for paper products. Tree farms are a good way to produce trees for harvest, but they are not useful to the spotted owl and other animals who have lost an old forest and are looking for another place to live.

As the tree farm starts to grow back, it is like an open meadow, with few or no hiding places. It will be used mainly by animals that burrow underground or are big enough to go out into open areas. Deer, for instance, might come out of the forest to eat the fresh young seedlings.

As the trees grow up, they will all be the same height and same age. After about twenty years, their branches will touch together and make a thick cover over the forest floor. Few plants will be able to grow in this shade. In one study, the number of animals that could use a tree farm at this stage dropped from twenty-eight down to nine. The spotted owl cannot use it. There are no old rotten trees for nests or open spaces where the bird can fly.

After sixty or seventy years, the tree farm people will decide that these trees are ready for harvest. But the animals that prefer older forests will think that these same trees have not grown nearly long enough.

If a forest is left alone to grow as it pleases, it will eventually become old and unique. Some trees will die or branches will weaken and fall to the floor. All sorts of insects and small animals will use this dead wood. Woodpeckers will tap into large dead trees to find insects and make a nest. When the woodpeckers leave, more birds and small animals will use the nesting hole.

Old-Growth Forest

This forest has many kinds of trees: old, young, alive, and dead. It includes open spaces where birds can fly, and soft, rotten logs where many plants, animals, and insects can live, hide, and eat. The soil is rich, thick, and full of nutrients.

Tree Farm

This tree farm is planted with one kind of tree and has no open spaces, snags, or logs. The forest floor is thin because it does not have much plant material falling into it to enrich the soil.

Meanwhile, the top of a tall tree might break off in a windstorm. The ragged, broken place will rot away to become another hole in the tree, and a pair of spotted owls will be able to use this as a nest.

Every time an old tree falls, it creates a large gap in the forest, allowing extra light to enter and a place for birds to fly. New trees will sprout up on the fallen log. If the log falls into a stream, it will attract insects for the salmon to eat and make deep pools of water where the fish can rest.

It takes centuries for these fallen trees to rot away. Meanwhile they provide shelter and growing space for thousands of plants and animals and return nutrients to the soil. Fungi help put these nutrients back into trees growing nearby. Flying squirrels will eat the truffles and spread the fungi all over the forest. And the spotted owl will eat the squirrels and live in the old trees until they fall over.

As the scientists discovered all these links between plants and animals, they realized something very important. There is nothing in an ancient forest that could be considered a weed, not even the dead stuff. It is a world woven together like a home-knit sweater. If one link disappears, all the places where it is connected might come apart too. They found value in everything, not because it can be sold, or hunted, or eaten, but just because it is an amazing, beautiful part of a natural community called an old-growth forest.

But many people think that trees are grown to be used and that logging has more value than the old forest. They do not like the spotted owl because the law that protects it has stopped the logging that they want to do. Right now, this bird is in the middle of a huge battle being fought over the trees.

4

Owls Versus Loggers

The fight over the trees has as many layers to it as the forest itself, but sometimes these layers have been buried under angry words and actions. Headlines in a newspaper read: OWLS VERSUS LOGGERS. TREE HUGGERS AGAINST TREE CUTTERS. KILL A SPOTTED OWL, SAVE A LOGGER. WAR IN THE WOODS.

This is the fight that people have heard all over the country. It is easy to hear all the anger and sadness involved. It has been very hard for timber workers to put away their chain saws, close sawmills, or park logging trucks in the street. On the other hand, it has not been easy for those who want to save the old-growth forests to watch the logging continue until ninety percent of the trees are gone. They have felt frustrated and unheard as they worked for seventeen years to get the spotted owl on the endangered species list.

There has been plenty of name-calling in the battle over the trees. Forest rangers, scientists, environmentalists, and loggers have all heard the shouting and at times have felt unsafe or uncomfortable. As the problems grew, the reactions grew too. The people who drove logging trucks rallied in huge groups, as many as twelve hundred at a time, to protest the loss of timber jobs. People in the communities showed their sadness and support by tying yellow ribbons to fence posts. One family in Washington was so devastated about the changes in their lives that they didn't have enough energy to open their mail for three months.

Logging trucks were seen with signs tacked onto loads of old-growth timber that said, MOBILE HOME FOR THE SPOT-TED OWL. Others drove by with bumper stickers. WE LIKE SPOTTED OWLS—STEWED, or IF IT'S HOOTIN', I'M SHOOTIN'. A few spotted owls have actually been shot and hung up for display.

Some environmentalists have also made extra-loud efforts to be heard. They chained themselves to trees and sat in the middle of roads to stop logging equipment. Some poured sand into the gas tanks of trucks and tractors.

An environmentalist sits on a sixty-foot high platform to protest the logging of old-growth timber along the Cedar River in Washington State. *Copyright Benjamin Nenschneider/Seattle Times.*

Hundreds of logging trucks in Kelso, Washington, rally against proposed cuts in timber harvesting. *Copyright Ted Thomas/Seattle Times.*

They have been arrested and even gone to jail. A few have pounded metal or ceramic spikes into trees, which is dangerous to loggers and millworkers, who might not see them and hit them with a saw.

Sometimes advertisements or articles have been written with confusing or incorrect information. Many people do not like to listen to these extreme ways to communicate. If they see twisted facts, dead owls, or sand in the logging trucks, they feel angry and afraid and aren't sure who to trust or what to believe.

But there are also many people in this battle who are trying to listen with some understanding and look for the facts that make sense. They are thinking about possible solutions to this huge problem. The group appointed by President Clinton to find a legal plan to protect the owl and still allow some logging received over one hundred thousand comments from all the people thinking about these issues.

Some people have looked for ways to use the forests carefully without logging the trees. Some are selling forest products that can grow back each year. These include berries and mushrooms to eat, and ferns and tree branches for florists. Millions of dollars worth of mushrooms are sold out of the forests every year. Others have set up businesses to guide tourists through the woods. Millions of visitors come to the beautiful national parks in the Northwest. If they stay longer and have more to do, it helps other businesses in the logging towns nearby.

Other people have said good-bye to lost timber jobs and are learning about new careers. Local colleges have

There has been plenty of name-calling in the battle over the trees.

hundreds of ex-timber workers studying about computers, engineering, and business. One man in Washington has learned how to shoe horses directly from a farrier in the community. The state of Washington is providing extra money for those who wish to take classes.

Some people are thinking about ways to repair the damage caused by heavy logging in the past. One the best ideas is to fix those thousands of miles of logging roads that have been slipping into the streams for many years. All this loose dirt smothers salmon eggs and makes the water muddy. Plans are being made to remove or repair some of the roads and turn others into hiking trails. These jobs will allow some ex-loggers to return to the woods. The work they do will also clean up the streams for the salmon. If more salmon survive, this will eventually lead to more jobs for salmon fishermen.

Every time a tree is cut, people are looking for the best ways to use the wood. They are thinking about everything, even the bark and leftover chips. Skinny trees that used to be burned in slash piles are now cut into thin strips and glued together to make broad panels. Small wood chips are pressed and glued into long boards. Some of these new products are sixty to eighty feet long, lightweight, and very strong. They replace the tall timber that is almost gone from the old-growth forests.

The newest sawmills, built for tree farm lumber, use computers to calculate the best way to cut each log with the least amount of waste. Then they send the logs past extra-thin blades that leave hardly a whisper of sawdust.

Every time people make an effort to stretch the use of a tree, it reduces our need to cut more trees. All of this is good for the spotted owl and the forest. Builders are using less wood and more steel and vinyl in new homes. Many families, schools, and workplaces are concerned about how much paper they use and are working to recycle more of it. Every time a ton of paper is recycled, it saves thirteen trees from a tree farm.

One community group helps woodworkers to find the limited wood that is still available and to share their supplies and equipment. Sawmills sell "waste" cedar to people who then use it to make wooden toys, bird feeders, and dog beds. One woman glues hundreds of small pieces of wood together to make bracelets. When she cuts out the middle section, another man buys this "waste" from her and turns the leftover pieces into beautiful doorknobs. Over three hundred small businesses are involved in this community network of working together.

Scientists have been looking at nature to come up with better ways to log trees. They are studying how a forest comes back after a fire and also learning about the return of the forests knocked down after the eruption of Mount

St. Helens in 1980. In both of these studies they have seen that nature does not destroy everything.

After a fire, the biggest trees with the thickest bark survive to reseed the forest. The area around Mount St. Helens has also benefited by downed logs and the few trees that survived. New ideas about logging include leaving the best old trees behind to reseed the landscape. In this way, new trees will sprout up that are just right for the location. Snags, logs, and other trees are also left behind for animals and birds and to keep the fungi that will help the new trees to grow.

Other scientists are trying different ways to help the tree farms look more like old growth. Some have replanted farms with a second type of tree. In some areas they have thinned and cut trees to create gaps and rotten wood. In other areas they have added wooden nest boxes or holes in tree trunks to create nesting places in young forests. All of these new tree-cutting methods could be good solutions because they allow some logging and still protect the owl.

But since scientists don't know everything there is to know about a forest, they might be missing something. We know how to trim trees and make nest boxes, but it is a very complex thing to grow a forest. This is why many people would like to keep as much old growth as possible, as the final places to enjoy and study ancient forests.

Even small amounts of old growth are not the same as

The Truffle Connection

The best ideas about logging include leaving enough trees and logs to maintain the connection between trees, animals, and fungi.

The flying squirrel lives in an old tree that grows with the help of a fungus around its roots.

The flying squirrel digs a round truffle to eat.

When the squirrel scampers through the forest, it spreads the fungus to other trees.

Roots with fungus and truffles

Roots without fungus

The fungus gets its food from the sugar in the trees.

The spotted owl lives in an old tree that grows with the help of a fungus around its roots.

The spotted owl flies down to eat the flying squirrel that eats the truffles and then spreads the fungus around to new trees in the forest.

A hemlock seedling will not grow longer than a year without the fungus.

Fungus with truffles grow with the tree roots and bring extra water and nutrients to the tree.

bigger areas. The edges of these small forests are more likely to blow over in the wind and be used more by bigger animals. It is hoped that the new tree-cutting methods will create better connections between small islands of forest so that owls can move from one place to another.

Studies of birds on islands show that if there are only a few birds in an area, they will disappear. But groups of thirty or more can survive for a long time. Also birds will sing much more often if other birds like them are around to listen. Spotted owls are talking birds too. They have developed thirteen ways to hoot, bark, and whistle because they have things to say. Some calls are an alarm for when hawks are in the area. Other hoots help the owls find a mate and a place to live. The newest ideas to help the owls include trying to create or keep large areas with many nests so the owls can communicate.

But knowing the needs of the spotted owl is not the entire answer to the problem of the owls versus loggers. If tree cutting is allowed that considers only the spotted owl, other rare and unusual creatures of the forest will be in trouble. The marbled murrelet, for instance, eats fish and cannot live more than fifty miles away from the sea. If we cut down large forests near the ocean because the spotted owl does not nest there, what will happen to the marbled murrelet? And what about slugs? They move so slowly that if they lose their home, they have little chance

Hearing the hungry cry of her owlets, a mother owl feeds her young. *Copyright Michael Ichisaka.*

to move somewhere else no matter how we cut the trees.

Does anybody care about slugs? Some people care a lot. A group in Oregon has asked the government to list several kinds of slugs as endangered. They want the tree-cutting plan to protect slugs too. The spotted owl is just at the top of a list of many valuable things in the forest.

5

❧

Skinny Trees, Slimy Slugs, and All the Rest of It

People have been studying the spotted owl and the ancient forests for about twenty years. This is not nearly long enough. How much time do we need? And what is it that we are likely to find?

Back in the eighteenth century, scientists were amazed to think that there might be as many as fifty thousand different plants and animals in the world. This sounds like a lot, but today we have identified and named 1.5 million different species. Many scientists think there might be millions more than that. With the help of new microscopes, computers, and satellites, they can see more details and layers to this world than ever imagined. It could take many years, many lifetimes, to learn about it all.

Scientists realize that some of these species will be limited to special communities, like rain forests, wetlands, prairies, and tundra. They also know that other species will be found in the unique world of the spotted owl. Already they have been amazed at the richness of their finds in the old-growth forests. One scientist saw two hundred and fifty different creatures in just one clump of soil. In the treetops they have found and named new spiders never seen before. They also found lichens, which are a combination of fungi and algae, that don't show up until the forest is well over a hundred years old. They even found some ants, high in a tree, that keep their own herd of aphids. Like they did for the spotted owl twenty years ago, scientists want to know more about these things.

When scientists have found time to study the world of the spotted owl, the results have been interesting. One example of this is the Pacific yew, the tree that the spotted owl likes to use for a perch. Some Indians use the wood to make bows and the needles to make medicine for the lungs.

For the last hundred years, however, the slow-growing Pacific yew was usually considered a weed. Some called it a "trash tree." It was one of the skinny trees that got bulldozed and burned as useless wood at the end of a logging operation.

But in the late 1960s, things started to change for the lowly Pacific yew. Scientists made a liquid from the red-

dish bark of the tree and called it taxol. To their amazement, this taxol was able to shrink cancer tumors in mice. They gave the taxol to cancer patients and saw that it was able to fight some kinds of cancer in people too. Suddenly they had an exciting product that grows in the old forests that could help tens of thousands of people who get cancer each year.

The Pacific yew was definitely no longer considered a weed. So many people went into the woods to collect the reddish bark that regulations were made to protect the tree. People who collected it illegally could be fined ten thousand dollars. Scientists learned that it took one hundred years of growing before the tree would contain much taxol. Then they discovered that it took three trees to get enough taxol for just one patient for one year. One hundred years to grow? Three trees for each person? They only had enough taxol for about five hundred cancer patients. Over a hundred thousand people were waiting for this compound. Now the yew tree seemed priceless and precious. Many cancer patients were not happy to hear that these trees had once been considered worthless and burned as trash. Scientists continue to look for the best way to make this compound in the laboratory.

A spotted owl hides on a low tree branch while hunting for food. *Copyright Tracy L. Fleming.*

Douglas-fir trees only produce seeds every 5 to 7 years. The yew provides seeds for birds every year.

Some birds eat the seeds of the yew and then spread them around the forest to grow new trees.

The spotted owl can use a low yew branch to cool off or to hunt.

Pacific yew

The Pacific yew likes the shade, moisture, and stable environment of an old-growth forest.

Pacific Yew Connection

The bark of the Pacific yew makes taxol, a medicine for cancer. It takes 12,000 yew trees to make 5 pounds of taxol.

TAXOL

In all this miracle medicine excitement, the Pacific yew is still the very same tree. It has always been an important plant to creatures in the forest. Birds eat the seeds, and elk and deer like to nibble on the foliage. For thousands of years, the spotted owl has often perched on its low branches as it sits and waits for something to eat.

But because we have had time to study it, we know that the tree is important to us, too. Nothing happened to change this tree except that we gained some new knowledge about it. A weed is only a plant for which we have not been able to find a good use.

Is this the only plant from an old-growth forest that has this kind of value? That is something no one can answer yet. Today more than a thousand compounds used in medicine come from other plants. Aspirin first came from the bark of a willow tree. Quinine, the treatment for malaria, comes from a tree in Peru. Periwinkle from Madagascar has saved the lives of thousands of children with leukemia. Penicillin comes from mold. A medicine for migraine headaches comes from a fungus.

Who knows what we will find as we continue to take a good look at the world of the spotted owl? Another interesting example is the slow, slimy creature called a banana slug. These slugs are found only in an old-growth forest, and they make a large amount of mucus wherever they travel. Scientists took the slug into the laboratory and watched this soft creature slink its way across the edge of a sharp razor without getting hurt. The only thing protecting the slug as it moved was the wet, gooey mucus between it and the razor. The scientists realized that this mucus must be a lot stronger than it looks.

With new instruments, they studied the mucus very carefully. They discovered that sometimes the mucus acts like a glue and sometimes like a lubricant and can change in a fraction of a second. Just as fast, it can expand five hundred times in size. Could this possibly be important? Well, our bodies are lubricated by mucus, including the eyes, nose, and lungs. When something goes wrong with this substance, we get sick. Scientists are looking at the secrets of slug mucus to help people with lung problems like cystic fibrosis. They are also using it to find better ways to deliver medicine to our bodies when and where we need it.

The silk that spiders spin is also being studied for clues. Some scientists are hoping to make stronger cable bridges by using the information that comes from a spiderweb. It may take just the right spider, as yet unstudied, to fill in the final pieces of this idea.

Other scientists are looking at the strong but lightweight exoskeleton of a beetle. It is a skin that protects and insulates and can stand a lot of damage. The beetle is helping us to build better vehicles. A compound from the mouth

A wet, gooey mucus helps the banana slug move, and also protects it from sharp objects. *Copyright Christopher Viney.*

of vampire bats is being used these days in surgery.

There are spiders, beetles, and bats in the world of the spotted owl. If we have the time to study them, one of these creatures might provide us with a clue that will make life better or safer in the future. Right now the salmon is being studied because in the last two weeks of its life, it ages as much as we do in twenty to forty years. We are hoping to learn something from this fish about the way we get old.

For every Pacific yew, we know that there are at least two hundred fifty thousand other plants. Only five thousand of these have been studied. For every salmon, there are at least nineteen thousand other kinds of fish. And we have no idea what is lurking about in the deepest parts of the ocean. For every spotted owl, there are nine thousand other birds. For every beetle, there are eight hundred thousand other insects. Some scientists estimate the total number of insects as thirty million, if we ever get around to counting them all.

Every time a species disappears, plants or animals that depend on it suffer too. When the dodo bird became extinct on the island of Mauritius, one type of tree there did not grow again for three hundred years after the bird disappeared. Then someone discovered that the dodo bird roughed up the seeds when it ate them and the tree was unable to sprout without this help from the bird.

All things are connected in ways that we can hardly imagine. Thirty years ago no one knew that fungi were helping the great trees around the spotted owl to grow. Or that the fungi got their food from sugars in the trees. Or that the flying squirrel and voles eat the fungi and spread it all over the forest. And that the spotted owl cannot survive without these connections that provide it with food and a place to nest.

The spotted owl has become the creature that allows us to talk and ask questions about everything in the forest. Does anyone know exactly why the spotted owl can fly

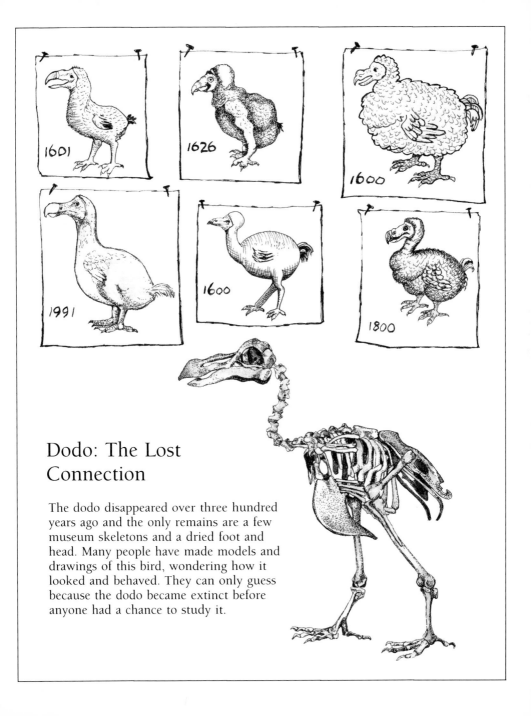

Dodo: The Lost Connection

The dodo disappeared over three hundred years ago and the only remains are a few museum skeletons and a dried foot and head. Many people have made models and drawings of this bird, wondering how it looked and behaved. They can only guess because the dodo became extinct before anyone had a chance to study it.

so quietly? Someday we might take a better look at owl feathers and develop them into the wings of our future. Because of the owl, we know more about flying squirrels. Has anyone taken a new look at this creature to understand how it can glide sixty feet down through the forest and land without injury? Does it have some special cushion in its legs that might be interesting to people with arthritis?

The spotted owl is our connection to a unique world in nature that has taken thousands of years to develop. Because we have learned about the owl, we also know more about banana slugs, fungi, the Pacific yew, and the marbled murrelet. And there is so much more. Vaux's swift, for example, probably the fastest bird in the world, is also trying to survive in the last of the old-growth forests.

The world of the spotted owl is like a library of books ready to amaze and inform us. We have looked at a few of the books, but there are rare editions on hundreds of shelves just waiting to be opened. These books belong to everyone and can be the knowledge of our future. With careful use, the old-growth forests can be there wherever we decide to take a new look at the home of the spotted owl.

Selected Bibliography

American Forests. September/October 1991: Vol. 97, Nos. 9 & 10.

Beyer, Don E. *The Totem Pole Indians of the Northwest.* New York: Franklin Watts, 1989.

Carey, Andrew B., and Wildlife Ecology Team, Ecosystem Processes Research Program. "Experimental Manipulation of Managed Stands to Provide Habitat for Spotted Owls and to Enhance Plant and Animal Diversity." Olympia, WA: U.S. Department of Agriculture, Forest Service, Pacific Northwest Research Station, 1993.

Christy, Robin E., and Stephen D. West. *Biology of Bats in Douglas-Fir Forests.* General Technical Report PNW-GTR-308. Department of Agriculture, Forest Service, Pacific Northwest Research Station, February 1993.

A Conservation Strategy for the Northern Spotted Owl. Portland, OR: U.S. Department of Agriculture, Forest Service; U.S. Department of Interior, Bureau of Land Management, Fish and Wildlife, National Park Service, May 1990.

de la Torre, Julio. *Owls: Their Life and Behavior.* New York: Crown Publishers, Inc., 1990.

Dietrich, William. *The Final Forest: The Battle for the Last Great Trees of the Pacific Northwest.* New York: Simon & Schuster, 1992.

Dittmar, Ann, David, Jane, Tom, Judy, and Steve. *Visitors' Guide to Ancient Forests of Western Washington.* Washington, DC: The Wilderness Society, 1990.

Durbin, Kathie. "From Owls to Eternity." *The Environmental Magazine*, March/April 1992, 30–65.

Ellis, Gerry, and Karen Kane. *America's Rainforest.* Minocqua, WI: NorthWord Press, Inc., 1991.

Facklam, Howard and Margery. *Plants: Extinction or Survival.* Hillside, NJ: Enslow Publishers, Inc., 1990.

Findley, Rowe. "Will We Save Our Own?" *National Geographic,* September 1990, 106–36.

Forsman, Eric D. *Methods and Materials for Locating and Studying Spotted Owls.* General Technical Report PNW-162. Portland, OR: U.S. Department of Agriculture, Forest Service, Pacific Northwest Forest and Range Experiment Station, 1983.

Forsman, Eric D., E. Charles Meslow, and Howard M. Wight. *Distribution and Biology of the Spotted Owl in Oregon.* Blacksburg, VA: Wildlife Monographs, 1984.

Franklin, Jerry F., and Thomas A. Spies. "Characteristics of Old-Growth Douglas-Fir Forests." Reprinted from New Forests for a Changing World Convention, 1988.

Jonas, Gerald. *The Living Earth Book of North American Trees.* Pleasantville, NY: The Reader's Digest Association, Inc., 1993.

Kelly, David, and Gary Braasch. *Secrets of the Old-Growth Forest.* Layton, UT: Gibbs Smith, Publisher, 1988.

Kirk, Ruth, with Jerry Franklin. *The Olympic Rain Forest: An Ecological Web.* Seattle: University of Washington Press, 1992.

Luoma, Jon R. "An Untidy Wonder." *Discover,* October 1992, 86–95.

Maser, Chris. *Forest Primeval: The Natural History of an Ancient Forest.* San Francisco: Sierra Club, 1989.

Maser, Chris, and James M. Trappe, eds. *The Seen and Unseen World of the Fallen Tree.* General Technical Report PNW-164. Portland, OR: U.S. Department of Agriculture, Forest Service, and U.S. Department of the Interior, Bureau of Land Management, 1984.

Mitchell, John G. "Sour Times in Sweet Home." *Audubon,* March 1991, 86–97.

———. "War in the Woods II: West Side Story." *Audubon,* January 1990, 82–121.

Norse, Elliott A. *Ancient Forests of the Pacific Northwest.* Washington, DC: Island Press, 1990.

Olympic Peninsula Product Buyers Guide. Port Angeles, WA: WoodNet Inc., 1993.

Pringle, Laurence. *Living Treasure: Saving Earth's Threatened Biodiversity.* New York: Morrow Junior Books, 1991.

Recovery Plan for the Northern Spotted Owl. Washington, DC: U.S. Department of Interior, 1992.

Sanford, William R., and Carl R. Green. *Gone Forever: The Dodo.* New York: Crestwood House, 1989.

Shepard, Esther. *Paul Bunyan.* San Diego: Harcourt Brace Jovanovich, 1952.

Tesar, Jenny. *Shrinking Forests.* New York: Facts on File, Inc., 1991.

Walker, Laurence C. *Forests: A Naturalist's Guide to Trees and Forest Ecology.* New York: John Wiley & Sons, Inc., 1990.

Watson, Jim. "The Last Stand for Old Growth?" *National Wildlife*, December-January 1990, 24–25.

Wildlife Vegetation of Unmanaged Douglas-fir Forests. General Technical Report PNW-GTR-285. Portland, OR: U.S. Department of Agriculture, Forest Service, 1991.

Wilson, Edward O., ed. *Biodiversity.* Washington, DC: National Academy Press, 1988.

Yolen, Jane. *Owl Moon.* New York: Philomel, 1987.

Zuckerman, Seth. *Saving Our Ancient Forests.* Venice, CA: Living Planet Press, 1991.

Index

Page numbers in *italic* refer to illustrations.

About the Author

Brenda Z. Guiberson is the author of several books for young readers, including *Cactus Hotel* (*Parents' Choice* Award), *Spoonbill Swamp* (NSTA-CBC Outstanding Science Trade Book), *Lobster Boat*, and *Salmon Story*.

While researching *Spotted Owl*, the author spoke to environmental groups, logging-industry workers, nature photographers, and local government officials to hear, in people's own words, the different sides of the spotted owl controversy.

Brenda Guiberson lives with her family in Seattle, Washington.